Spiritual Breadcrumbs
from the Universe
Insights Into A More Meaningful Life

Jim Brown

authorHOUSE®

AuthorHouse™
1663 Liberty Drive
Bloomington, IN 47403
www.authorhouse.com
Phone: 1-800-839-8640

First published by AuthorHouse   07/15/2011

ISBN: 978-1-4567-6664-1 (sc)
ISBN: 978-1-4567-6665-8 (ebk)

Library of Congress Control Number: 2011907072

Printed in the United States of America

Also by Jim Brown

A Rose Garden—Living in Concert with Spirit

Getting Things Done—Keys to a Well Balanced Life, with Jack Canfield

To my beautiful wife, Rosemarie. Words can never express my gratitude for a lifetime of your love, devotion, and loyalty.

Contents

Acknowledgments

Let me start by thanking the spiritual teachers who have been sent to me since I published my first book, *A Rose Garden—Living in Concert with Spirit*, in 2005. First and foremost is Karen Anderson, who taught me to recognize my spiritual gifts and trust myself. Shannon Lee Faulkes significantly raised my vibration during our brief time together; it was extraordinarily powerful. Laurie Anderson is currently expanding my consciousness into worlds I was previously unaware of, including animal communication, extraterrestrials, spaceships, our lineage, the earth and sun having souls, spiritual lightning, to name a few. Thank you, Laurie. Marydale Hahn taught me about love through yoga. To all of you, thank you for sharing your spiritual gifts with me and with everybody who ventures into your world. The world vibrates at a higher level because you are here being your God selves. Namaste.

Preface

Spiritual Breadcrumbs from the Universe- Insights into a More Meaningful Life contains over three hundred thoughts, questions, and bits of wisdom. My goal is for these breadcrumbs to provide you with spiritual food for thought. Take them into your heart and allow those that resonate with you to nurture you and heal your wounds. Let the rest go. We have all been hurt. Allow these "spiritual breadcrumbs" to heal you and return you to your state at birth; a place of unconditional love and hope.

I have been a motivational speaker since 1991. I've spoken predominantly in the healthcare field and on cruise ships. I talk about change more than any other topic. What I've learned, as a result of speaking about change over one hundred times, is that we are all creatures of habit. If you think I'm trying to change you or teach you something, you will shut down. My passion as a speaker and author is to share with you another way to perceive your life experiences. Use whichever "spiritual breadcrumbs" resonate with you, as tools in your growth process.

This brings me to how I came up with the title "Spiritual Breadcrumbs from the Universe." Every one of us gets lost on the road of life from time to time. In *Hansel and Gretel,* the children follow breadcrumbs to lead them home. We have spiritual breadcrumbs to guide us back onto the trail of connecting with and becoming one with our Creator. I use the word "Universe" to identify our Creator. You may use a different word, such as God, Yahweh, Allah, Source, Spirit, or any other number of other words. What's important to me here is the concept of becoming one with our Creator, our God, our Source, our Universe. I get lost in this journey often. An important resource for me is the cards from *A Course in Miracles.* I've quoted several of them in this book. I believe totally in divine synchronicity. Therefore, it's my belief that all of the spiritual breadcrumbs are here to assist us on our journey back to our God, our Source. The Universe is providing us the spiritual breadcrumbs we need to nourish our spiritual growth and development.

I will tell you what I tell every audience and most people I meet. I only have a point of view. Be true to yourself.

The fact that you have this book in your hands is part of divine synchronicity. The other part of divine synchronicity is for you to read these spiritual breadcrumbs and allow them to speak to your heart. Then allow your intuition to guide you to action. Keep this book as a resource throughout your life. Every time you pick it up you'll be in a different place in your life and each breadcrumb will have a different meaning.

Open the book to any page and let it talk to you. Ask a question and the book will open to the answer. Divine synchronicity is a gift that works every time we use it. My intent is for this book to provide you with another way of seeing things that aren't working in your life. Be sure to give a copy of this book to everyone you love who will be inspired by these breadcrumbs. I hope this is a book you will want to give to your friends as a gift.

This book is in your hands today because you are ready to begin or continue the journey back into wholeness. Use it as a road map to bring you back onto the path of self-discovery, self-exploration, and self-love. With these gifts, you will reach out to everybody in joy and love.

As you continue your life journey, remember that there is nobody God loves more than you. You're the only person

God has ever created with the gifts He gave to you. Please share your unique divine gifts with the rest of us.

Every night, I have a slice of frozen triple-chocolate cheesecake from Jenny Craig. I let each piece melt in my mouth. I do this in order to enjoy the chocolate longer. I have found that this philosophy is a great one to use in all areas of my life. This savoring process creates a delicious dance. Savor each one of these thoughts to see how they can bring you back into balance and harmony.

At the end of the book are some pages for you to record the "breadcrumbs" you want to keep. Copy these keeper breadcrumbs and carry them with you as a reminder.

Use the white space on each page to answer questions or make comments.

Section One: Matters of the Heart

When I am able to express myself from my heart I share from who I really am. I share my higher self, my soul. When I don't share from my heart, my ego usually runs the show and starts judging, criticizing, withholding, questioning, doubting, being scared, feeling alone, feeling inadequate. My goal in this section is to show you the path from your head to your heart. Hopefully, when you are finished, you will be more comfortable expressing from your heart more often.

When you are comfortable being true to yourself and your heart, you'll live a life that's much freer. Your power is knowing who you are and loving yourself for who you are, not for what you have or what you do. When you accomplish this, you'll no longer seek validation from others. You will accept that it is safe to express from your heart, because you will no longer need others to validate you.

Take your time exploring the concepts in this section. Come back to them often.

1.
Love

What if the purpose of our life is to learn how to love? First we have to learn how to love and accept ourselves just the way we are. For most of us this means we are going to have to adapt new beliefs about ourselves that will replace the limiting, critical, judgmental, not good enough, beliefs we have bought into. As you read this chapter, look for "breadcrumbs" you can use to new create beliefs about yourself.

Next we have to learn how to love others just the way they are. It's easy to love somebody when he or she loves you back. The challenge is when others are angry, hostile, belligerent, or arrogant. What if they didn't love themselves and believed that they didn't deserve to be loved? What if they behaved so poorly that it would be nearly impossible for you to love them? Then, in their mind, when you don't love them, they are right! They don't deserve to be loved. Very few of our parents knew how to love themselves. Therefore, they couldn't teach us, their children, how to love ourselves.

Where do you go to learn how to love yourself? Hopefully you'll find some ideas in this chapter. How would your life change if you believed your purpose in life is to learn how to love yourself and others just the way they are?

You cannot live in fear and love at the same time. When you find yourself in fear, ask God to immediately remove you from this fear and transport you back into the world of love. Close your eyes and see God coming for you, instantly removing you from fear and gently placing you back into your inheritance of love.

Fill the air around you with love. Send it out in front of you, so everywhere you go is always filled with love.

You are safe. Do not allow any emotion, pain, or scars from the past stop you from living in the fullness of your heart. Expressing love is the essence of who you are. When you love, give your love freely, as a gift, without any expectation of how this gift is received or used. Give love purely for the great joy you experience as a giver of love. You have done this with a newborn baby. You gave this precious child all your love and expected nothing in return. This innocent baby taught you how to love in purity. Take this precious gift and share it.

Love yourself just the way you are.

When people misbehave, they may be saying, "I am not worthy of being loved," or "I don't deserve to be loved and I'm going to prove I'm right by behaving so repulsively you won't love me." Choose instead to love them, simply because they are. They don't need to earn your love. This is unconditional love.

If I had one wish, it would be that everybody loves himself.

A Course in Miracles says we are doing one of two things: giving love or asking for love. We sometimes disguise asking for love as anger, resentment, jealousy, envy, withdrawal, or by being demanding. See through people's disguises and give them the love they are asking for when they are expressing themselves fearfully. You may just be sending love from your heart to their heart.

Love yourself just the way you are and it will be easy to love others just the way they are.

Life is a dance. What kind of dance do you want your life to be? One of love, joy, compassion, and patience, or one of anger, revenge, and hate? It's your life, so choose your dance partner well.

Write a note to somebody you love, explaining how much you appreciate her or him.

When babies have temper tantrums, we pick them up, hold them to our bosom, and comfort them. If an adult you know is having a temper tantrum, similarly envision yourself holding him to your bosom, comforting him, and loving him.

Treat yourself like you are number one. Learn how to nurture yourself first. You are most valuable when you come to a situation with a full tank—that is, rested and nurtured.

Love is the flame that lights your heart. It has value only when it is shared. Use the loving light within your heart to relight the heart light of one who has forgotten how to love or how to be loved. Use this heart light to brighten the heart light of another who is having trouble loving himself.

Bless everyone you meet, everywhere you go.

Let go of all the lies that your ego has deceived you into believing. When you do this, the fog created by these lies lifts, revealing a beautiful, loving being whose purpose is simply to find a creative, spontaneous way of being loved and loving others.

Jim Brown

God never created anybody that He loves more than He loves you!

There is a small child within you who has not been nurtured and loved enough. It doesn't matter how old you are, because nobody has ever been nurtured enough or loved too much. Pick up this child and hold her to your heart and reassure her that she is loved, and that you will nurture her for the rest of your life.

Dr. Gerald Jamplowsky wrote a book titled, *Love is Letting Go of Fear.* We are challenged to let go of our fears. We should lead our life from a place of love rather than from a place of fear.

Many people believe that the purpose of life is to win the game of Monopoly. That is, many people live their lives as if all that matters is the acquisition and possession of material goods (money, houses, cars, boats). What if the purpose of life is to learn how to love ourselves and others, even when it is difficult?

Heal the pain of somebody not showing you an act of love by loving yourself. You are whole and complete just the way you are.

What do you have to believe to accept yourself just the way you are? See yourself as a work of art in progress.

Before we are born, we live with God at home in a world where only unity and unconditional love exist. We ask God if we can run an errand for Him. God agrees to let us leave our perfect home to run this errand of love. Then we are born. This is like walking out of your front door. Once you leave the safety and comfort of your home, you don't know what elements you'll meet while you are gone. We meet many others who are also on errands, and they may be lost and scared. Remember, they are your beloved brothers and sisters. Don't be fooled by what they look like, how they are dressed, or how they behave. The further they get from home, the more they forget who they are and why they are here. Do whatever comes to you, intuitively, to comfort them. Show them love, compassion, patience, acceptance, and tolerance.

Nobody has ever died from an overdose of love.

Most everybody I have ever known struggles with the inability to set boundaries and enforce them. I think we are afraid of hurting other people's feelings. Boundaries are a statement of self-worth. You are telling people, "This is how I want to be treated." The easiest time to set boundaries is in the beginning of the relationship. You deserve to be treated with dignity and respect. Are you ready to attract people into your life who will treat you with dignity and respect?

Experiments have proved that food prepared with love tastes better.

What if, when you got behind the wheel of your car, your job was to send love out in all directions to every person you see? Once you love doing this, expand it into another area until it fills your whole life.

Let's play Jeopardy. The answer is, "Love." The question is, "What is the solution to every problem?"

Love the child that is still inside of you, no matter how old you are.

Learn to live in your heart.

Newborn babies are 100 percent dependent upon us.
And they are the easiest to love. Why do you suppose
that is?

What do you love about yourself?

The past is gone, and the future will never get here—
the present is all you have. That is why it is such a
beautiful present. Embrace the present as a divine
gift of love.

Elizabeth Barrett Browning wrote a poem called, "How Do I Love Thee?" Give yourself a great gift and write your own poem or letter saying how you love yourself.

God loves you unconditionally; that is, there is nothing that you can ever say or do that will ever change God's love for you!

You can't say or do anything to deserve God's love. God's unconditional love is your birthright.

Do you find that you are your hardest judge? How would that change if you loved yourself more?

You're always safe. Visualize yourself being embraced by God, and feel God's heart encasing you completely with unconditional love!

Chances are the child within you hasn't been loved enough. How do you want to show your child within that it is loved?

What one thing will you take from this book that will make your life more loving?

2.
Happiness

It is my belief that everybody wants to be happy. I believe this is a universal truth. The question is, *how* can I be happy? My answer is that you must release your expectations. If you have no expectations for yourself, for life, or for other people, then you cannot be disappointed. A major reason people aren't happy is that life hasn't fulfilled their expectations. Another reason people aren't happy is that they look for things outside themselves to make them happy. Some examples are a successful career, money, a spouse, children they are proud of, a big house, expensive cars, boats, vacations, clothes, a certain weight, physical beauty, and prestige.

How much happier would you be if you were happy with who you are rather than what you have? Don't wait for something to happen to be happy—just be happy. As you read this chapter, pick at least one "breadcrumb" that you believe will create happiness in your life.

Jim Brown

It's better to be happy than right.

Smile. It's contagious.

Laughing makes everybody feel good. Look for what is funny in every situation.

Try to get one person to say to you every day, "You made my day."

The key to happiness is releasing your expectations. If you have no expectations for yourself, or for anybody else, or for any situation, then it is impossible to be disappointed by anybody or any situation. You are always happy when you have no expectations!

A key to a happy life is being true to yourself.

Whenever I see an engaged couple or a newlywed couple, I share my belief about how they can be guaranteed to have a happy marriage. I tell them to tell their spouse every day what they love about them. This forces them to look for what they love in their spouse rather than their faults. Imagine how your relationships would change if you looked for what you love in every person.

Happiness is contagious. Spread it everywhere you go.

Every night before you go to sleep, tell yourself the most beautiful thing you saw that day, heard that day, experienced that day, or read that day. This will get you in the habit of seeking beauty everywhere you go. This practice will change your life.

Listen to Joe Cocker sing "You Are So Beautiful" as if God is singing this song to you.

Which is more important to you, to judge and condemn, or to forgive and be happy?

As I mentioned in the preface, my favorite food is Jenny Craig's triple chocolate cheesecake. I eat it frozen and let it slowly melt in my mouth. My tongue dances with each bite. If only I could have this relationship with everything I eat. Then eating would be a divine dance. By savoring each bite, or anything else in your life, you are engaging in a magnificent divine dance with your Source. What are some favorite things or people you savor?

Make a list of the beliefs you need to let go of to be happy.

I watched a TV show about Siegfried and Roy. It documented the tiger mauling Roy and his subsequent recovery, which took five and a half years. At the end of the duo's farewell show, Siegfried said, "Look for the magic that is around you in nature, plants, flowers, and all the animals with which we share this planet. Look for it and it will lighten your heart and your life." Look for the magic. You will find what you look for.

3.
Forgiveness

For many people, forgiveness is an insurmountable mountain. Why? Well, it's my point of view that forgiveness becomes nearly impossible when we set ourselves up as judge, jury, and executioner. We have deemed that somebody has done something that is unforgivable. How heavy is the burden of judging and condemning? I'm not saying that behaviors shouldn't have consequences. But forgiveness is about releasing the emotional attachment to the event. This in no way condones the behavior. In my opinion, forgiveness has nothing to do with the offending behavior. **Forgiveness is only for one person—you.** For most of us, the hardest person to forgive is ourselves. If you want to get deeper into this than we cover in this book, I recommend Louise Hay's book, *You Can Heal Your Life*. She also has an accompanying workbook.

Forgiveness is a process, not an event. You may have to forgive somebody for days, weeks, or months before you are totally free of the emotional attachment. Once I had to send love to somebody every day for nine months before I was freed from the emotional attachment to the event! Remember, the purpose of forgiveness is to release yourself from the emotional attachment to the event. Forgiveness is like getting out of jail. Forgiveness frees you from the burden of judgment. To me, it is better to be happy than right. Skip this chapter if you're not open to forgiving yourself or others. However, if you are willing to open your heart to forgiving, then read this chapter with the intent of finding the tools that will allow you to forgive. For when you forgive, you will find peace, wholeness, and healing.

Forgiveness starts with you. Forgive yourself.

I knew a woman whose son had been run over and killed by a man traveling with several other men in a car. During the manslaughter trial, she stood up in the courtroom and forgave them! If she could do that, what grudge are you ready to let go of, or what hurt are you ready to release so that you can heal? Remember, forgiveness is releasing the emotional attachment to the event. Forgiving is in no way condoning behavior.

Forgiveness is letting go of the emotional attachment to the event.

All of us do the best we can with the resources available to us at any given moment. There are days when you feel unstoppable and days when it is nearly impossible to get out of bed. Forgive everybody who hurt you because they didn't have access to love, compassion, or understanding at the moment they said or did something that hurt you.

You can never heal the pain from any emotional wound while you are holding on to it. Now is a great time to release this pain so that you can begin the healing process.

Forgiveness is giving up all hope for a better past.

Jim Brown

Make it a daily practice to let go of your emotional attachment to the past. Every day, forgive yourself for all the mistakes you have made in this lifelong experiment in Earth school. Every day, let go and let God.

Today is the day to forgive yourself for everything you perceive you have done wrong.

When you are meditating, imagine that one by one, everybody who has ever offended you comes to you saying, "Please forgive me for everything I have ever said or done to you that has hurt you in any way!" Feel your burden lift, and feel your heart healing and becoming whole again. When you are ready, imagine that there is a line of people in front of you. Say to each one of them, "Please forgive me for anything I have ever said or done that has hurt you!" When all of this is complete, you all join hands in a circle and a huge white ball of light encircles everybody and replaces the hurt with love. Feel the energy of this love being passed to you.

Every one of us has been hurt. All of us need to heal. A huge step in healing is forgiving your past.

Holding on to the pain of the past is like carrying one hundred pounds of rotting garbage with you everywhere you go. Love yourself enough to let go of this huge burden.

What if forgiveness healed every malady? Would you use it?

Who is the hardest to forgive? Yourself or others? Forgive the hardest one first, and then the others will be easy.

Jim Brown

How does it serve you to judge somebody as wrong
and carry the pain of that judgment around with you
for your entire life?

What if all you have to do to be happy is to forgive
and forget?

4.
Heart

We live in a society that values matters of the mind or intellect almost exclusively. As a consequence, few of us have learned how to live in our hearts. To compound the problem, when we opened our heart, loved, or became vulnerable, often somebody abused this sacred trust and broke our heart. The pain was so intense that we shut down our heart, built a brick wall around it, and determined that we would never love or trust again. This creates a very unfulfilling life.

Our challenge is to learn to live life balanced between our heart and our head. Just as our physical heart is the source of our physical body's life, so is our emotional heart the source of our emotional life. I want to live a life worth living, and to do that I must live from my heart. I have to love, forgive, let go, surrender, start over, build, grow spiritually, heal, and keep giving openly of all my God-given talents and gifts. If my heart is shut down I have nothing to give! Life is amazing, it's beautiful, and it's filled with joy and happiness. We must open our heart to let this joy, happiness, love, forgiveness, and beauty out so others in our life can return it. Give your love freely! As you read through this chapter, look for ways to live from your heart more often.

I am at the door of your heart. I try to open the door, but it is locked. I ask you to give me the key to unlock your heart and let me in. Why won't you let me in? What do I have to say or do to gain entrance into your heart?

What are you afraid will happen to you if you let me into your heart? This is your fear. What do you have to believe to dissolve this fear?

Give from your heart.

Have you ever suffered paralysis from analysis? I believe overanalyzing things can cause us to become paralyzed. Generally, we're paralyzed with fear. When I feel paralyzed, I stop analyzing and go from my head to my heart and trust my heart, my instinct, my gut. The eighteen-inch journey from your head to your heart is the longest journey you'll ever take.

When a friend's dad was dying, I suggested that she create an altar in her heart. Now she has the opportunity to create memories with her dad that she can cherish for the rest of her life. When you get the opportunity to assist somebody you love in making the transition from this life to the next life, what are the memories you want to savor and cherish in your heart? What do you need to say or do to create these memories? Don't be intimidated by the past. Your goal is to be sure that you will have no regrets after your loved one passes. What do you need to forgive the person for? What do you need to be forgiven for? What do you need to say you are sorry for? Life here on Earth is a sacred gift. Your loved one is a gift to you. Be sure you wrap this gift in a way that you will treasure it for the rest of your life.

What if you were to send out one hundred thank you notes? Whom would you thank and what, specifically, would you thank them for?

Look in the mirror, through your eyes, and into your heart and soul. See there the incredible beauty of the real you. Here lives the essence of life. Dust off this beautiful, loving being, and feel the light of your incredible heart shine forth and well up from within, quickly lighting your entire being from the inside out. Allow this image of yourself to become your guiding light.

I believe that one of our key challenges is to live in balance, and one of the key areas to balance is between the head and the heart. Most of us are extremely comfortable and experienced living in our heads. Our society doesn't encourage us to live in our hearts. Yet it is when we live in our hearts that we are connected to our highest truth and to each other.

Hear God speaking to you. What would Mother God say to you? What would Father God say to you?

How do you get into your heart? I close my eyes, shut off my brain, and see and feel myself drop into my heart.

Imagine that you are going to have a dinner party and can invite anybody you want from all of history (those living in body and those living in spirit). When they come to your party, what do you want to talk to them about? Have this party. It will take place either in your mind or in your heart. Where will you have a better time?

Your heart wants to talk to you. Go someplace quiet where you won't be disturbed, and ask your heart what it wants to say to you. Then trust everything that comes to you.

If there is somebody in your life who is an adversary or thorn in your side, send love from your heart to his or hers. Do this as often as you need to until the relationship shifts.

Jim Brown

Within your heart, there's a huge bright light called your soul. Open your heart and invite your soul into your life.

What if your peace lived in your heart? Would you go into your heart more often?

You are beautiful! Look in your heart and see and feel that beauty lighting up your heart. Now let your face and body become the mirror of your heart and reflect this beauty out for everybody to see and feel.

If I ask you what you feel about something, how do you connect with your feelings?

God walks into your heart and gives you a gift that will heal you and make you whole again. What is this gift?

Imagine God saying to you, "My sweet child, I love you so much and I'm so proud of you." Then God tells you all the amazing things, great and small, you have said and done!

5.
Common Sense

Either common sense isn't common, or people don't use their common sense very often. I am sure that you will find at least one breadcrumb in this chapter that you can incorporate into your daily life.

Common sense isn't common.

Some people say they don't trust anybody. These people then drive on a two-lane highway with two yellow lines painted down the middle of the road. They never question if the yellow paint will keep an eighteen-wheeler on his side of the road. To me, expecting a yellow line to keep a truck on its side of the line is big-time trust.

Life is a process, not a series of events.

Develop a clear sense of who you are. Know that you are a spiritual being who is a physical expression of Source. When you know who you are, then you can choose to respond to life circumstances from the point of view of who you are (a physical extension of Source).

I find that stories are a great way to get your point across or teach something.

There is no such thing as reality, only perception. You are the only one who creates your perceptions. Therefore, your perceptions create your reality. If your life isn't the reality you want, change your perceptions.

See change as a vehicle that gets you through life.

Stop seeking the approval of others. Approve of yourself just the way you are. Your validation or sense of value should come from within, not from the opinion of others.

Jim Brown

I think our lives would be a lot more fulfilling if we lived every day as if it were the first day of the rest of our lives rather than just another day.

You cannot live until you overcome your fear of death.

If you were to put all of your thoughts and comments into either a positive bucket or a negative bucket, how much bigger would the negative bucket have to be? If you recognize your negative thoughts and replace them with positive thoughts, your positive bucket will get bigger.

Change your thinking and change your life.

If you try to give me guilt, and I refuse to accept this guilt, who still has it? Never let anybody else make you feel guilty!

Mother Earth is the source of our bodily existence. She provides us with air, water, and food. Respect the source of your physical existence with love and honor.

Incorporate into your day committing one random act of kindness.

Which area of your life is most out of balance? What one action will you take today to bring it back into balance?

Jim Brown

Connecting to God is like plugging your computer into an electrical source, turning it on, and then going to the tutorials to learn how to use this amazing resource.

If ignorance is bliss, why aren't there millions more blissful people?

6.
Family and Friends

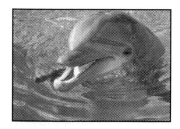

Here is where the golden rule applies: treat everybody the way you want them to treat you. Reducing life to its lowest common denominator, my belief is that life is about relationships. And those relationships are with our Creator, our family, our friends, people we interact with on a daily basis, and ourselves. In this chapter we will focus on family and friends. We have all had problems with our family and our friends. Hopefully, you will find a "breadcrumb" or two in this chapter that will enhance your relationship with your family and your friends. Of course, all of these "breadcrumbs" can be applied to yourself and those who pass through your life on a day-to-day basis.

If you want a friend, be a friend.

Take off your costume of fear, resentment, pain, withholding, intimidation, anger, and aloneness, and stand in front of a mirror and behold the beauty of your true essence: a Divine spiritual being who has disguised herself in a physical body. The masquerade ball is over. Take off the costume and reveal the real you to the world. When you reveal the real you, you are, in effect, giving me permission to reveal the real me.

Babies give you four gifts:
>   1. They love you unconditionally.
>   2. They forgive and they forget.
>   3. They have no idea of failure.
>   4. Everything they do is an adventure.

What would your life be like if:
>   1. You loved unconditionally?
>   2. You forgave and you forgot?
>   3. You had no idea of failure?
>   4. Everything you did was an adventure?

If your parents were never taught how to love themselves, they couldn't teach you how to love yourself. Forgive them for not teaching you something they didn't know how to do!

All of us come from dysfunctional families. Our parents did the best they could with the resources they had available to them at the time. Now we must accept responsibility for our own lives.

When I was a kid, my mom used to say to me, "Honey, someday you will understand." I think this is God's mantra to us, all day, every day.

A friend is somebody who would rather be anywhere else than with you and is with you anyhow.

Day-Old Child
My day-old child lay in my arms,
With my lips against his ear.
I whispered with emotion,
"How I wish that you could hear."

"I have a hundred things to say
(A tiny cough and a nod).
Hurry, hurry, hurry, and grow
So I can tell you about God."

My day-old baby's mouth was still.
And my words only tickled his ear,
But a kind of light passed through his eyes,
And I saw this thought appear:
How I wish I had a voice and words.
I've got a hundred things to say.
Before I forget, I'd tell you of God—
I left Him yesterday.
—Author unknown

Bling, glory, and joy accompany the events of one's wedding day. Much time and money is spent preparing for a one-day event, while the process of building a marriage is often sorely neglected. Maybe that's why half of all marriages end in divorce. Learn how to be married. Marriage is an ongoing growth process.

Your children learn from watching what you do, not what you say.

Jim Brown

The greatest gift you can give your children is to tell them they can do whatever they want to with their lives or be whoever they want to be.

When your children misbehave, let them know that their behavior has consequences—and you love them! They are not their behavior. Never teach them that they must do something to be loved and never withhold your love from anybody.

What are your top five values? How do you know when they are being honored? Share these insights with your spouse or partner.

If mom and dad are alive, thank them for everything they have given you.

7.
Compliments

There is nothing easier to give than a compliment. Often this compliment makes a person's day and in some instances changes his or her life. I love to hear somebody tell me, "You made my day," when I give a compliment. It is so much fun to see the glow on another person's face. This brings joy to my heart. When you read this chapter, put on your rose-colored glasses and begin a journey of finding ways to compliment everybody you meet. I promise you that if you do this it will change your life.

I love playing with people and bringing smiles to their faces. For example, I will ask an older couple if they are on their honeymoon. Usually one of them will say, "Yeah—fifty-seven years!"

Promise yourself to give someone a compliment every day.

Whenever I see a woman whose hair is beautifully combed, I ask if her hair wakes up in the morning looking so beautiful. If she has a man with her, I will ask if she brought her personal hairdresser with her.

At Christmastime, when two siblings are together in a restaurant, I tell them that I am one of Santa's helpers and that when I get home, I'm going to e-mail Santa and tell him how good they are being. Not only does this bring smiles to their faces, but it also brings a smile to their parents' faces.

When your server does a great job, tell the manager.

When I see a child in the store with a parent of the opposite sex, I will ask the child if that's her husband (or his wife). Usually, they say, "No, that's my daddy," or, "That's my mommy." It's so much fun to see the looks on their faces.

When I see a child in the store with a parent, I'll ask, "Which aisle did you get that beautiful child in?" Often, the parent will tell me she's the last one.

Another thing I'll say to a cute little kid is, "How did you get so pretty? Do you take beautiful pills?" Again, what a joy it is to see the look on the child's face and his or her parents' faces.

You're a diamond in a mine. Your job is to chip away at the rough edges and expose this beautiful diamond. Then polish yourself for all of us to see your glorious beauty.

Self-doubt is not a gift to humanity. Please stop doubting, judging, and criticizing yourself. You are beautiful just the way you are.

Make a list of things you have done in your life that you are proudest of. Then read it every time you're feeling down or depressed.

8.
Attitudes

It is often said that your attitude determines your altitude. In Section Two of this book there is a chapter on choices. One of our choices is to choose our attitude every moment of every day. We cannot control what goes on every day, but we can control our attitude or how we choose to respond to the situation. And one choice is to choose to respond with love—the way we would like to respond when we are at our very best. Your attitude will have a huge impact on the quality of your life. And your attitude will, in many instances, dictate the attitude of others. Choose to have an attitude that will always be for the highest and greatest good of everybody concerned.

Your attitude determines your altitude.

The first insight in *The Celestine Prophecy* by James Redfield is that there are no coincidences. I agree totally with this. If you believe in coincidences, you've discovered another way to give up your power. If you see that everything is divinely choreographed for your highest good, your life will undergo a miraculous change.

There is a famous story about Thomas Edison. He was trying experiment after experiment to invent the lightbulb. After five thousand failed experiments, one of his staff came to him and said, "Tom, you are a failure."

Tom said, "What you mean?"

"You have failed five thousand times."

Tom responded, "No, I have discovered five thousand ways not to invent a lightbulb."

Now, what would your life be like if every time you did something that didn't give you the outcome you desired, you said, "I have discovered another way not to make it work"?

Henry Ford said, "If you think you can or think you can't, you are right."

The value of our differences is one of the most magnificent ways we have to teach other people the power of our uniqueness.

Everybody makes a difference. The issue isn't whether we make a difference or not; the issue is whether that difference will be a positive or negative difference.

I went to college with a guy who used to say, "It's better to break your arm patting yourself on the back than it is to break your leg kicking yourself in the bottom."

Dr. Wayne Dyer suggests that we don't die with our music inside us. Do everything you want to do in your life so that on the last day of your life you don't have any regrets.

Ask people to help you get what you want. Motivational speaker Zig Ziglar says you will get what you want when you help enough other people get what they want.

What is a world record? It is doing something nobody has ever done before in all of human history. What do you think the mindset of that person was before he or she set the world record? What does your mindset need to be to accomplish something you may consider to be impossible?

Jim Brown

"If you aren't enjoying the journey, chances are you won't enjoy the destination." (Joe Tye)

In 1953, an article appeared in a medical journal asserting that it was anatomically impossible for a human being to run a mile in less than four minutes. In 1954, Roger Bannister ran the first sub-four-minute mile. Within one year, twenty-six more men had broken the four-minute mile.

Self-esteem is the reputation you have with yourself.

A Course in Miracles says, " ...when any situation arises which tempts you to become disturbed ... say 'There is another way to look at this.' If the way we're looking at something doesn't bring us peace and happiness, then we need to ask, 'How else can I see this?'"

One night after having my pupils dilated at the ophthalmologist's, I was driving and all the lights were blinding. When I saw taillights, I slowed down. I learned two things from this experience. One, I should have taken a cab home. Two, you never know what is going on in the life of the person behind the wheel of another car. Therefore, when somebody is driving in a manner that upsets you, rather than getting frustrated, show compassion.

One Saturday afternoon, I was touring Yellowstone National Park. The road in Yellowstone is a two-lane road with no shoulders. The next day I waited until the very last moment before I left for the airport. I ended up behind somebody who was touring, and I realized that his agenda that day had been my agenda on the previous day. Therefore, I was patient rather than frustrated.

Jim Brown

At the end of every day, ask yourself, "What is the best thing that happened to me today?"

Do you live in a friendly world or hostile world? I live in a very friendly world.

One of my favorite quotes from *A Course in Miracles* is, "If you knew who walked beside you on the path you have chosen, fear would be impossible."

You deserve all the abundance life has to offer. Believe that you deserve an abundant life and express constant thanks and gratitude for all the abundance you presently have in your life.

What if you believed everybody you see is your roommate and your role is to create harmony?

What if everything you believe about yourself and your life (your story) isn't true?

9.
Faith

We all have faith in somebody. In this chapter we will primarily focus on our faith in our Source, God, the Universe, or whatever word you are most comfortable with. To me, the major focus in our life is to always work on developing our relationship with our Creator. Pick up the "breadcrumbs" in this chapter that will enable you to have a deeper and more unconditionally loving relationship with your God. One of my beliefs is that all roads lead to God. Some roads are bumpier and more fraught with danger, but nonetheless they all lead to God. You are on the right road.

If God brings it to you, God will bring you through it.

I love the prayer "Footprints in the Sand." In the last line, God says, "When you only saw one set of footprints, that was when I was carrying you." Close your eyes and picture yourself climbing onto God's back. Now wrap your arms around His neck, wrap your legs around His waist, and see Him carrying you through every difficult situation in your life.

Most people believe in God. Our challenge is to trust God. Trust that everything that happens in your life happens for your highest good and the highest good of everybody involved.

Trust yourself, trust God, and trust the process of life.

Jim Brown

Hope is the ability to see a better future. Hope is impossible if you try to see it through the trials of the past. Hope grows in strength when you surrender the need to figure out how you will have a better tomorrow. You must believe you will have a better tomorrow without any evidence to support this belief. This belief is predicated on the ability to trust that your Creator will fulfill your hope as a gift to you. This gift cannot be earned. It is freely given to those who open their arms and hearts.

Once, while I was giving a talk, the idea of hiring God as my chief financial officer came to me. He took the job! The problem was, I was a terrible supervisor. I assigned God the job of ensuring we were financially secure. However, I kept challenging Him, saying, "Where's the money? How come I don't have it yet?" In other words, I didn't trust God to do the job of being God! If you choose to hire God to be your chief financial officer, tell Him everything you want Him to do, and then trust Him to do His job.

When I did my first fire walk at a Tony Robbins seminar, he said that the fire walk was just a metaphor. He said, "If you believe this is impossible, and I can show you that it isn't, what else is there in your life that you believe is impossible that may not be?" After I did the fire walk, I stood there in total disbelief. I remember thinking, *If this man can get me to do this, what can I do if I put my belief in God?* What can you do that you think is impossible, if you surrender into the hands of God?

Life is preparing to go to the Olympics. Olympians devote their entire lives preparing for the Olympics. Then the day finally comes when they go to the Olympics and live their life dream. When you die, you realize your ultimate dream of being reunited with your God, your Source, or your Creator. This is like going to the Olympics and getting a gold medal.

If you feel separate from God, who left?

My favorite prayer is "Let go, let God."

I love the serenity prayer, which says:
God, give me the courage to accept the things I
cannot change,
The strength to change the things I can change,
And the wisdom to know the difference.

Once I had a problem that was creating an enormous amount of pain for me. While in a bookstore, I picked up a book and opened it to a page that was the answer to my pain and provided me with peace. To me, this was a miracle or an answer to my prayer. When we pray for help, we should look for the answer everywhere we go.

If you have one prayer, let it be "Thank you."

Jim Brown

This is a prayer that came to me in meditation:

Love brings you peace.
Peace leads you to your sacred spirit within.
Sacredness expands your ability to give and receive love.
Expanded love leads to an infinitely expanded sense of peace.
This expanded sense of peace enhances your sense of the sacred, which opens your heart and soul to receive unconditional love.
Having your heart and soul open to unconditional love leads you to infinite peace, which connects you to the heart of the sacred where all love resides!

Section Two: Matters of the Mind

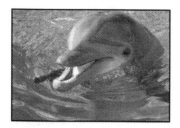

In this section you'll find breadcrumbs to assist you in your day-to-day interactions with the world. One of the presentations I give to groups is about the balance between your professional and your personal life. One of the points I make is that we spend a huge amount of our time focusing on what is urgent in our life rather than what is important. Take a few minutes to jot down the five most important areas or relationships in your life. Now, write down how much time you spend a week in each of these five most important areas of your life. Where do you want to make adjustments?

10.
Advice

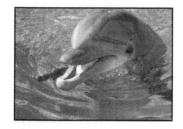

In this chapter, I would like to share with you some of the things I've learned as I've traveled through the journey of life. If any of these resonate with you, jot them down in the back of the book, where there's space for you to create a customized list of your favorite spiritual breadcrumbs.

Listen with compassion.

Life is not a competition. There is nothing to win. We are all winners, because we chose to participate in Earth school. Relax, you win; you will graduate from Earth school. Enjoy the lessons from your teachers. The curriculum, called your life, was designed for only you, so you are not competing against anybody else for anything. There is no value in comparing yourself to anybody else.

Life is a masquerade party. Everybody is wearing a mask. Really, what we have is God dressed up and disguised as a drunk, a murderer, a rapist, your boss, your problem child, or whoever else is giving you problems. Hopefully we can say, "Good one, God. You fooled me for a while. I thought you were a jerk, and it really was You."

Never put anybody on a pedestal.

You developed your beliefs to get you through a particular period of your life. When you got past that challenge, you no longer needed those beliefs. Therefore, at least once a year, review your beliefs about life and ask yourself if these beliefs still serve you. If not, replace them with ones that do.

Whenever anybody tells you anything, run it through your truth meter. Ask yourself, *Does this resonate with me as being true for me today?*

Live your life in such a way that when you die you will have no regrets.

When you were a kid and your parents asked you what you wanted for your birthday, did you worry about whether they could afford it or how they would get it? Probably not. You simply accepted that you would get what you asked for without understanding how it would happen. Your job now is simply to tell the Universe what you want and let the Universe decide how and when it is going to get it to you.

Always focus on what you want, not on what you have or what you don't want.

Your feelings belong to you. They are neither right nor wrong. When your feelings have been hurt, say, "My feelings were hurt by that remark. Was that your intention?" Don't say, "You hurt my feelings," because that causes a person to become defensive. We all say things unintentionally that are hurtful.

You are always being guided. Listen to this guidance.

As you move through your day, find creative ways to make people you meet feel good about themselves.

God has a container that stretches from here to infinity. Each one of us decides what size container to take from this infinite supply of abundance. The only requirement is that you believe you deserve it.

Make a list of things you want to do, people you want to meet, and places you want to go. Post this list someplace where you will see it every day, and make it your life's work.

"If it is to be, it is up to me" is a great quote from William Johnson. It inspires us to take action and not wait for others to do something.

At Senator Ted Kennedy's funeral, Father Dan Coughlan said, in part, "Competition can be converted to collaboration."

If today is the last day of your life, what is the legacy you want to leave behind? Now start living your life in such a way that you create this legacy.

In Miguel Ruiz's book *The Four Agreements*, my favorite agreement is the second one: never take anything personally.

Never withhold your love. It's like holding your breath. Hold it long enough and you will die or pass out. When you get upset, stop and take several deep breaths to bring yourself back to a calm state.

Talk to yourself the way you would talk to your best friend or the person you admire most in all of history.

Somebody once told me, "That which I am seeking is seeking me!"

Spend time everyday telling yourself what you are grateful for. Some even keep a gratitude journal.

When you get trapped by negativity, become aware of where you are and start moving toward love. What's the first step in that direction? Maybe it's going from being angry to being peeved.

When you ask the Universe for something with intention and attention, release it to be delivered in the Universe's time, not yours.

If you don't toot your own horn, somebody else might think it's a spittoon.

Isn't it fascinating how we find wonderful things to say about people at their funerals? Say these wonderful things to them while they are still alive. Tell them what your favorite memories of them or experiences with them are.

When we are kids, the bogeyman lives in our closets or under our beds. When we become adults, we think there is no more bogeyman, but actually the bogeyman moved into our heads. He scares us into believing the worst-case scenario will occur. Shine your light on this dark perception and know that all is well.

Keep a list of things others say or you read that really have value to you. Read this list when you need help seeing things from a higher point of view.

Make a list of how you are blessed and read it every day or whenever you are feeling bad.

Instead of asking people how they are, ask them, "What is the best thing that has happened to you in the last week?" or, "What are you grateful for?"

When you're having a pity party for yourself, decide when your party will be over, and then get on with your life.

Jim Brown

Make a list of your gifts. Don't be humble. Read this list whenever you need to feel better about yourself.

When you give a gift, give it without any expectations of how it will be received.

Write a letter to somebody and tell that person the impact he or she has had in your life.

Keep it simple, sweetheart (KISS).

Be careful what you ask for; you may get it.

Beware of anybody who says there is only one way to do anything. There's always another way.

11.
Choices

We always have choices in life. However, sometimes we get stuck. When we get stuck, we no longer see the choices available to us. The purpose of this chapter is to give you a variety of choices that are available to you in almost every situation in life. The key is to remember them when you need them. Choices create freedom. The belief that you have no choice will always keep you stuck. When you are stuck, you are living in the past with no hope of the future being any different. In order to create a future that is different from your past, you will need to make different choices. If you don't, your life will be like the movie *Groundhog Day*, where every day was exactly the same. My major goal in this book is to give you tools that will empower you to live a fulfilling life. Choice is one of the biggest tools that you have to get what you want out of life and be who you came here to be.

There is no limit to the number of times you can choose. If you don't like the results of a choice, choose again.

When somebody comes to you in anger, you can choose how you will respond—with anger, love, kindness, or compassion.

Everything you say and do creates an outcome. This is either an outcome you want or an outcome you don't want. If it's an outcome you want, then duplicate the action, like a cookie-cutter, and continue to get this desirable outcome. However, if it's an outcome you don't want, you must change something in the process until you get the outcome you want. Remember, insanity is doing the same thing over and over and expecting a different result!

When you make a mess in your life, clean it up. That is, make it right.

Everybody has a center. Mine is sacredness. Yours could be peace, calm, integrity, love, or happiness. Whatever it is, keep a symbol that serves as an anchor to remind you of your sacred center so that when you stray, this anchor will remind you to come back to your center. I carry a stone in my pocket to remind me.

Instead of judging, practice observing.

You are the only person who has control over what you think. Therefore, you must become the gatekeeper of your mind. When you recognize that you are having a negative thought, do your job as a bouncer and kick the negative thought out of your mind.

Jim Brown

Instead of criticizing, try feeling compassion.

We are huge magnets. We attract into our lives whatever energy we are putting out. Usually we are thinking about what we have, not what we want. Therefore, we will get more of what we have, which is usually what we don't want. To have the life of your dreams, you must always be thinking about the way you want your life to be, not the way it is!

You are the only person ever created that has been given the gifts you have. Please share them with us.

The past is a perception that only exists in your mind. The great news is that you can always change your perception of a past event. Look for another way to see it.

There are no victims, only unconscious creators.

Esther Hicks, author of the best-selling book *The Law of Attraction*, tells us that everything we want in life is downstream. She advises us to stop paddling upstream, and let the stream of life bring us everything we want.

How would your life change if you surrendered the need to control outcomes?

So often, something is said or done that elicits a spontaneous reaction. Usually that reaction is negative. Instead, let us see it and choose how we want to respond to this word or event in the future. Program yourself to respond the way you choose to when you are responding from your highest state of being.

Jim Brown

Change your definition of failure to, "I am a failure only if I don't try." Now every time you try, you'll be a success.

When we change the way we think, our lives will change.

My favorite definition of worrying is, "paying interest on a loan you never received."

To me, stress is the difference between how your life is and the way you think it should be. If life is going the way you want it to go, there is no stress. When things don't go the way you think they should go you experience stress. The bigger the gap between the way life is and the way you think it should be, the greater the stress.

Surrender yourself and everything that occurs in your life every day, all day, to God.

One of my speaking programs is titled "Stress is a Point of View." I believe this is 100 percent true. Nothing, absolutely nothing, causes stress. The cause of stress is the way you choose to perceive the event, not the event itself.

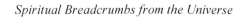

Focus your energy on what is important in your life, not on what is urgent.

Energy follows thought. Negative energy always follows negative thoughts.

When you are in a stressful situation, ask yourself, "What would I have to believe for this not to be stressful? What would somebody who is not stressed by this situation believe?"

What does the word "no" mean to a two-year-old? Nothing. If "no" doesn't stop a two-year-old, don't let it stop you.

Your life will be much more fulfilling, satisfying, and gratifying if you accept yourself just the way you are. Once you can accept yourself the way you are, it is easy to accept others the way they are.

To paraphrase Shakespeare, life is a play and we are all actors. If you don't like your role in life, choose another one.

Jim Brown

Beauty is in the eyes of the beholder. Behold beauty everywhere you go.

Freedom is a state of mind. What prisons have you created in your mind by your limiting beliefs?

When you are in a stressful situation, how does your body tell you it is being stressed?

Here's a great reason to make a conscious effort to recognize when you are thinking negative thoughts and expel them immediately. **A negative thought will never create a positive thought or a positive belief!**

I met a woman who fostered twenty-four children. One of them was a lesbian, and this mother's religion condemned lesbians. Thus this mother felt that she couldn't love her daughter. I asked her to give me her written resignation as the general manager of the Earth. She did. Then I gave her permission to love her daughter and her religion. We always have choices, and love is always the choice.

Ralph Waldo Emerson said, "Life is a journey, not a destination."

Terry Cole Whitaker wrote a book whose title had a great influence on my speaking career. It is *What You Think of Me is None of My Business.* This gave me permission to be myself and accept that you have the right to think of me however you choose.

We are brainwashed into believing that happiness is found in things like clothes, cars, money, and liquor.

When you are in a stressful situation, the most important thing you can do is to nurture yourself. However, that is usually the last thing one thinks about doing when one is stressed. Make self-care your first priority.

Today you get to decide, for you, who God is and what your relationship to God is like. Oh, and every day is today.

12.
Life Lessons

It is my point of view that we have come to live on planet Earth to learn lessons. Everything that happens to us in our life is here to teach us a lesson. Therefore, everybody who comes into your life comes to teach you something. *A Course in Miracles* says there is another way to look at this. This chapter on life lessons is intended to give you another way to look at things that happen in your life. You will never stop learning lessons. The key is to learn your lessons easily and in the minimum number of times. That is, you don't want to have to repeat the same lesson over and over and over again until you finally get it. How nice it would be if we could learn the lesson the first time it is presented to us, rather than having to go through frustration and aggravation before we finally get it. The goal in this chapter is to find a breadcrumb or two that will help you learn your life lessons easier and faster.

My favorite quote is from the Foundation for Inner Peace's book, *A Course in Miracles*. It reads, "What could you not accept if you but knew that everything that happens to you, past, present, and to come, is gently planned by One whose only purpose is your good?" What that means to me, is, what couldn't I accept if I knew everything is a gift from God? The question causes me to ask, *How is this a gift?* Continue to ask this question until you get an answer.

Life isn't fair!

Life is a school. We all come to Earth to learn lessons. Therefore, our entire life in Earth school will be spent learning lessons. We will have some magnificent teachers. Some of the teachers are love, problems, relationships, careers, disease, money, change, children, spouses, adversity, prosperity, accidents, fear, and anger. Our challenge is to recognize these gurus when they present themselves in our lives and ask them what they have come to teach us. Often when we have problems, we deny them, drug them, overeat, drink, or engage in other self-defeating behavior. The key here is to recognize that we have created this experience to learn a lesson and grow. If we don't learn the lesson through this experience, we will be provided another opportunity to learn this lesson. **Nobody, nor any part of life, is without lessons.**

Jim Brown

The people in your life have come into your life to teach you something. And you are in their lives to teach them something. Therefore, whatever situation you're in, ask yourself, *What is she here to teach me?*

Life is a mirror. People reflect back to you unresolved issues that you cannot see inside yourself.

Seek the higher, deeper meaning to everything.

Cause is internal; effect is external.

Life is a process. At a Tony Robbins seminar I attended, one of our tasks was to climb a sixty-two-foot telephone pole. I interviewed a woman who had climbed the pole. She told me she climbed the pole, stood on top, jumped and caught the trapeze, and was down in one minute and twenty-eight seconds. My reaction was, *I can beat that time.* Then somebody told her that that must be how she leads her life—she never enjoys the process. In twelve days the biggest lesson I learned is that life is a process, not a series of events. What do you have to believe to enjoy the process of life?

A friend told me, "*Why* is the booby prize." How many times have we asked ourselves, "Why did this happen to me?" A better question might be, "What is this experience trying to teach me?"

My favorite song lyric is, "Let there be peace on Earth and let it begin with me." Seek peace in anger, hostility, and negativity. Find the peace in the chaos.

Jim Brown

When my wife and I were approaching our fortieth anniversary, I remember my mom saying, "A lot of people are married forty years, but not many are married fifty years." I got scared, thinking that we may have less than ten more precious years together. Through prayer and meditation, I worked through that fear and changed it to a resolve to enjoy every day I have with my beautiful wife, Rosemarie. I am steeped in humble gratitude for the gift of this incredible love. Cherish your relationships.

"Look up; get up; never give up," Michael Irvin.

In my opinion, life is a scavenger hunt. We come into this world with a list of things we are to do, see, experience, learn, and grow from. It doesn't matter when you get the things on your list done; it may be the second you left heaven or the second before you get back. Our challenge then is to see how many of our experiences we learn from.

Life is a series of experiments. The failed experiment is as important as a successful experiment. We learn so much from so-called failed experiments.

The most valuable lesson I have learned from speaking is that I can play with people. Everywhere in the world I go, I play with people and they always play back. Go play with people.

When we can remove our emotions and egos from our life experiences, we can then observe every experience as a lesson.

Life is a constant series of adjustments.
The more you adjust, the more you learn.
The more you learn, the more you grow.
The more you grow, the more you become divinely connected.
The more divinely connected you are, the more you will grow.
The more you grow, the more you will learn.
The more you learn, the more you will adjust.
And the beat goes on in the circle of life!

What if the only things you could take out of this life were your memories? How would that change the way you live? How would it change your relationships?

Life is a process, not a series of events. Be gentle and loving with yourself. You will make mistakes your entire life. This is part of being human. The key is what you learn from these mistakes.

It's not what happens to you that matters, it's what you do about it.

The external events in our lives are the means by which we learn the internal lessons that we came into this world to learn.

In November of 2001, I gave a talk titled "The Gifts From 9/11." I opened with this story:

> Imagine yourself in the most magnificent ballroom you've ever seen. In walks your Creator. He says, "I need three thousand volunteers to be born all over the world. You will all come to the United States, and on September 11, 2001, you will all die. However, because of the way you die, the whole world will think about how important it is to love, to have compassion, to tolerate others, to honor and respect people regardless of their color, their race, their religion, or their beliefs. Would you volunteer to have your life stand for this?

I took a class that met one weekend a month. In February, we met in the cold and snow. They told us to bring our bathing suits, because there was a great spa outside. I couldn't imagine walking outside in the snow in a bathing suit, getting wet, and then walking back to the lodge in the cold and snow, but I decided to take a bathing suit anyway.

One group decided they were going to do an exercise around the pool. I put on my swimsuit, clothes, and jacket, and walked out to the pool. As part of the exercise, we were figuratively throwing all of our dreams into the pool. Then we took off our clothes and went into the pool, into our dreams. The fact that this pool was heated to 106 degrees didn't lessen my anxiety one bit.

The fifteen to twenty seconds I stood barefoot on that cold cement in the snow, I experienced the most excruciating physical pain of my life. It was like standing on a bed of nails. I walked to the ladder and descended into the pool, and began to experience the most remarkable transformation of my life. The 106-degree water brought a complete sense of calm and peace. The experience of the snowflakes dancing on my face and head and fluttering into my eyelashes felt like a dream. Had I let my fear of being cold stop me from going through with that experience, I never would have reached the ecstasy of being in a pool in the snow for the first time in my life. Face your fears. Never let fear deprive you of the opportunity to have a beautiful experience.

I've spent much time pondering why we are here on Earth. In *Blessings from the Other Side,* Sylvia Browne says, "When we plan our lives, we are given a choice of seven option lines to choose from: love, health, finance, career, spirituality, family, and social life. The option line we decide on is the area of this earthly school that we've decided to major in, the area we'll agonize over the most, and the area we feel we have the most to learn."

Tony Robbins taught me that life is a series of memories, and the best gift you can give to another person is creating a memory for that person.

Life is a continuous series of adjustments. Buddhism refers to this as "impermanence."

What is the most valuable thing you've learned in your life?

The way to know if your internal dialogue is coming from your ego or from your higher self is the following: if you are disturbed, the dialogue is coming from your ego; if you feel peace or it feels good, it is coming from your higher self.

Develop a ritual that brings you back into the state of peace whenever you lose this peace.

You don't have to accept every invitation to an argument.

What if your story of limitation isn't true?

13.
Challenges

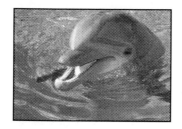

Life will always be filled with challenges. The key is to have strategies that will enable you to meet these challenges, to conquer these challenges, and to learn your life lesson from these challenges.

You'll find only what you look for. Now go buy a pair of rose-colored sunglasses and look for only the good in people. I promise that you'll find it in everybody.

When you find yourself in a difficult situation remind yourself that **this too shall pass**.

My uncle once said, "Some people think this is old age, when in reality it is adaptability." It seems that "adaptability" could be a tagline for all of us to follow. We are constantly challenged to adapt to the ever-changing circumstances in our lives. Our challenge is to adapt with grace.

Learn to live in the eye of the tornado, where there is complete calm.

Everybody I have asked agrees that no two people see life exactly the same way. Most of us just want others to respect our viewpoint, not to convert to it. The logical extension of this scenario is to respect everybody else's point of view. We will all always be different from each other. Our challenge is to learn to live with and get along with each other in spite of our differences. We must learn that killing each other because of our differences will never solve our problems.

My chapter in the anthology *Getting Things Done—Keys to a Successful Life,* co-authored with Jack Canfield, is about life according to me. It is my belief that each one of us has an unwritten list of how life works in every area. When people disappoint us, it is because they have violated one of our rules for how life works. And we never even told them that this is one of our rules for how life works. Our challenge here is to release our expectations for how other people should live their lives.

You change only when you get sick and tired of being sick and tired.

Albert Einstein said no problem can be solved from the same level of consciousness that created it.

When something frustrating happens—somebody cuts you off on the freeway or says or does something to upset you—say, "I don't want to get into that energy."

Have you learned how to dance the dance of being a gracious receiver? Many of us (especially moms) are great at giving to others but struggle at receiving. What if when somebody complimented you, gave you something, or paid for something, you viewed it as a gift from God?

How can you bring more peace into your life today?

Eckhart Tolle tells us that whatever we resist persists. Thus our challenge is to recognize when we are resisting something and become aware that as long as we resist this it will continue. Next we are called to surrender and let go of what we are resisting.

Define all the elements of your problem, and then stop giving your problem any more energy. Instead, give all of your energy to the solution.

Do you know that if you pour a goldfish out of a nine-inch-diameter bowl and into a bathtub, it will continue to swim in a nine-inch circle? Which of your beliefs is causing you to swim in a nine-inch circle, when you could be swimming in a bathtub, a lake, or an ocean?

If today were the last day of your life, what would you say to the people around you?

In the early 1950's, Wilma Rudolph's mother wheeled Wilma in a wheelbarrow to see a doctor. The doctor told her that Wilma would never walk. Her mother refused to believe the doctor and massaged her daughter's legs every day. Eventually she walked. Then she ran. Then she won three gold medals in track in the 1960 Rome Olympics.

If you were told that the person you love most in life had just died, what would happen to your body? Your mind gave meaning to the words and the meaning you gave to these words triggered hundreds of chemical reactions in your body. The point is that your mind has control over your body. You can also use your mind to heal your body.

When you believe you're a victim, you're giving your power up to the situation at hand. What are some of the ways you give up your power?

One reason some people have problems when they retire is their identity is directly related to what they did for a living. When they don't do it anymore, they don't know who they are. And worse for some, their self-worth is related to their work. See your value in who you are, not what you do.

What are the benefits you are deriving by staying stuck? Look for negative benefits. Everything we do in life serves us somehow—even if it is negatively.

Native Americans have a saying, "Walk a mile in another man's moccasins." The next time you're having a problem or an issue with somebody, try to see the situation from that person's point of view. In other words, try to defend his or her position.

Life is a series of experiments. The failed experiment is as important as a successful experiment. We learn so much from "failed" experiments.

Whenever you have a problem in life, whether it is physical, mental, emotional, or spiritual, put a chair in front of you and sit the problem in the chair facing you. Ask this problem what it has come into your life to teach you. You must listen for the answer and trust that what you hear is the truth.

I love Frank Zappa's quote, "A mind is like a parachute. It works best when it is open." Sometimes it is a challenge for me to remain open.

I am a genie. I will give you one wish. What is it?
Now that you know what you want for yourself, let
me tell you how to get it. First, you must believe you
deserve it. Second, stop trying to figure out how this
could possibly happen. Third, you must vividly see
your wish arriving. When doubting thoughts arise,
you must expel them with the same sense of urgency
you'd have about finding water if your hair was on
fire.

Visualize your life as perfect just the way it is now. This will necessitate dropping certain beliefs and judgments about yourself and your life.

You have exactly what you believe you deserve to have in your life. If you want more in some area of your life, then examine the limiting beliefs you have in that area and create more expanded beliefs.

14.
Affirmations

Affirmations are simply positive statements phrased in the present tense to enable you to create the energy, the attitude, and the determination to live the type of life you deserve.

Muhammad Ali used to say, "I am the greatest." Say that out loud, and then listen to the self-talk. Which will you believe? If you chose to believe the self-talk, you'll stop saying, "I am the greatest." However, if you continue to tell yourself "I am the greatest," you will quiet the self-talk.

All life is sacred, and I consciously acknowledge the sacredness of life and myself and every human being. I promise to treat all life as sacred.

My book *A Rose Garden—Living in Concert with Spirit* contains the following affirmation: "God is the source of my power. He lies within me, and I know that all my power lies within me, that all wisdom and all answers are within me. I willingly retreat within myself for the answers to all the questions in my life."

I embrace my life as a physical experience with God on Earth. I allow every other human being to live his or her life as a physical expression of God.

I am mentally, spiritually, and physically flexible and embrace my flexibility as a sign of my openness to receiving God's love into my life.

My life is a living testament to my being a Divine being in a physical body. I invite the Divine presence of my Creator to work in and through me every moment of my life.

My divinity is expressed and experienced through the values by which I choose to live my life.

We usually think of a blessing as something holy that is given to us by a cleric. Yet when we sneeze, people say, "Bless you." How about if you bless yourself every day with this blessing, "I bless myself with peace and love, now and forever. And so it is."

15.
Some Points of View About Life

This chapter is a compilation of tidbits I've picked up. I hope they will help you live the kind of life that you deserve to live. You're an amazing person who needs to learn how to love yourself just the way you are. You deserve all the abundance life has to offer. Believe it and claim it as your birthright.

Abundance is your birthright. Claim it.

Create a vision of how you want your life to be. Envision every detail. Use all of your senses. Be passionate about it. Be sure this is a creation that is for the highest good of all. Now release this creation to the Universe to be fulfilled. You must also release your need to know how this could possibly occur. Your part in the process is complete with the creation of the vision.

Abundance is a state of mind, a way of being. There are millionaires who don't have abundance and paupers who are filled with abundance.

What is the most important thing you want to be remembered for? Are you living your life in such a way that this is what you will be remembered for? What do you want your legacy to be? Begin to live that legacy today.

Part of abundance is learning to receive gifts that are given graciously without feeling that you are beholden.

If you seek revenge, dig two graves—one for yourself.

One day I was talking to God, and when I heard Her response, I thought, *That's just my imagination.* Then I heard God say, *What better place is there for Me to meet you than in your imagination?*

When you get upset, stop and take several deep breaths to bring yourself back to a calm state.

My trinity is balance, integrity, and love. What is yours?

Keep a list close by of everything that is sacred to you. Every day, pick one person or thing that is sacred to you and focus all your loving energy on her, him, or it.

Some of my favorite trinities are the following:

Peace, acceptance, and love

Peace, grace, and blessings

Love, wisdom, and compassion

How is this world a better place because you live here?

As you watch the sun setting, somebody else is watching it rise. In our society, we see death as a sunset. In the spiritual world, a person making his or her transition is seen as a glorious sunrise.

God has been trying to give you a gift, but you keep refusing it, saying, "I don't deserve it; I'm not worthy." Receive this gift in total gratitude, love, and trust. What is the gift God wants you to have?

I am a human being, not a human doing. Therefore, I set aside time every day to simply be.

Hillel the Elder says, "If not you, who? If not now, when?" This seems like a great philosophy to live by.

Practice graciously receiving gifts from others, whether they are physical gifts or acts of service.

You are a gift to everybody you meet. Share the gift of you, so that your world is a better place because you are here.

Don't take life for granted. Appreciate everything you have in your life, big and small.

The only truth is what is true for you today. You're evolving; therefore your truths will change.

The process of life is about loving, giving, forgiving, receiving, learning lessons, having fun, playing, letting go, grieving losses, being present, seeking, and growing.

If you are better at giving than receiving, make a conscious effort to receive everything that is given to you with gratitude.

Adversity reveals the person; it does not define the person.

You are never alone.

Life is not about judging, criticizing, condemning, belittling, or abusing.

Abundance is a state of mind.

My Keeper Breadcrumbs

My Keeper Breadcrumbs

My Keeper Breadcrumbs

Congratulations for having the perseverance to read this whole book. Now, before you put it down, make a copy of the breadcrumbs that you listed in the back of this book. Read this list and pick out one that you promise to implement in your daily life.

Thank you for the opportunity to come into your life. I hope your heart has been touched and opened wider. From the depths of my heart I send you my love and my healing energy. It is my deepest desire that you heal and become whole again.

All my love,

Jim

About the Author

Jim Brown MBA is the coauthor with Jack Canfield of "Getting Things Done - Keys to a Well Balanced Life" and author of "A Rose Garden - Living in Concert with Spirit". Jim has his MBA from Loyola University of Chicago and his BA from Loras College in Dubuque Iowa. He has been a full time professional speaker since 1991. He lives with his wife Rosemarie in the Los Angeles area. His web site is WWW.JIMBROWNSPEAKER.COM

You may purchase this and other titles directly from
Author House at www.authorhouse.com
Click on the last tab on the right–bookstore to order
additional copies of this book.
Or call author house toll-free at 888–519–5121
Or order the electronic version
Or go to Amazon.com or BN.com
If you would like more information about Jim's seminars
go to WWW.JIMBROWNSPEAKER.COM